Shadow Work

Demystifying the Psychology Behind Self Discovery, Inner Work, and the Healing Journey

> *"Freud was content to investigate the basement of the house. I want to explore the whole building."*
> *~ Carl Gustav Jung*

By

Jason A Solomon, B.Ed

Title: *Shadow Work: Demystifying the Psychology Behind Self
Discovery, Inner Work, and the Healing Journey*
Author: Jason A Solomon, B.Ed
First Edition: 2025
ISBN: 978-1-7638935-6-6
Cover design and interior layout by Aussie Guy's Books

This is a work of nonfiction. Names and identifying details may have
been changed to protect individual privacy.

"One does not become enlightened by imagining figures of light, but by making the darkness conscious."
~ *Carl Gustav Jung*

Shadow Work AI Companion

Your shadow journey doesn't have to end when you put the book down. To support deeper reflection and personal exploration, you now have access to the **Shadow Work AI Companion** – an interactive guide built around the same principles of Jung, Freud, and the evolving practice of shadow integration.

This tool is designed to help you:

- Ask personalised questions about shadow work, inner healing, and self-integration
- Receive thoughtful, reflective guidance in real time
- Explore journaling prompts, emotional triggers, and archetypal patterns in more depth
- Continue your practice privately, at your own pace

Simply scan the QR code below:

Use it as a companion while reading, or return to it whenever you need a mirror for your inner journey. Thousands are already using AI to illuminate their shadow self - this is your chance to join them.

Preface

Shadow work is not a modern invention. Long before hashtags like #InnerWork or #HealingJourney trended across digital platforms, the human psyche was already wrestling with its disowned reflections. What we now call the "shadow" is not an enemy to be defeated ~ it is a mirror turned inward. It contains everything we have rejected, repressed, or been taught to abandon: our rage, our shame, our hunger, our wounds ~ and yes, even our brilliance.

This book is not a guide for therapeutic healing, nor is it a workbook filled with mantras or journal prompts. Instead, it is a psychological map ~ a structured, accessible resource for understanding the inner terrain that lies beneath our polished, performative lives. It offers a clear-eyed explanation of what shadow work is, where it originates, why it matters, and how it shapes our emotional, relational, and cultural patterns.

The philosophical roots of this book are grounded in the pioneering work of Carl Gustav Jung, the Swiss psychoanalyst who gave language to the hidden self. Jung introduced the concept of the shadow to describe the unconscious and often morally neutral parts of our personality that the ego refuses to acknowledge. Unlike Sigmund Freud, who viewed the unconscious primarily as a repository of repressed childhood desires ~ especially sexual and aggressive impulses ~ Jung saw it as a vast inner landscape that also contains creativity, wisdom, and unrealized potential.

Freud believed the psyche was driven by conflict between instinct and societal repression, and therapy aimed to uncover these buried drives to relieve neurotic suffering. Jung, in contrast, viewed the unconscious not just as a source of pathology, but as a partner in the process of becoming whole. He introduced concepts like the anima, animus, persona, and Self ~ emphasizing the symbolic and spiritual dimensions of the mind. For Jung, personal growth was not merely about catharsis or symptom relief, but about individuation: the lifelong journey of integrating the conscious and unconscious parts of the self.

"One does not become enlightened by imagining figures of light," Jung wrote, "but by making the darkness conscious."

To Jung, wholeness was not about perfection, but integration. He believed that healing comes not from erasing our contradictions, but from embracing them. When we ignore or exile our shadow aspects, they act out in distorted or unconscious ways. But when we turn toward them with awareness, the shadow becomes a guide rather than a saboteur. It holds the raw material for authenticity, sovereignty, and depth.

This book carries Jung's vision forward. In the decades since his work emerged, thinkers and clinicians have expanded upon his foundation, blending analytical psychology with trauma theory, attachment science, somatic awareness, and neurobiology. Today's shadow work reflects a growing understanding of how human beings fragment under pressure ~ and how, in the presence of safety and insight, we can gently reclaim what was once denied.

You won't find formulas or prescriptions in the chapters ahead. What you will find are frameworks, language, and reflective insights designed to illuminate the hidden architecture of your inner world. Whether you are an educator, therapist, seeker, or someone quietly navigating your own becoming, this book is here to demystify the shadow ~ not to fix it, but to understand it.

Because understanding is not only the beginning of integration ~ It is a radical act of self-honesty.

And that, in Jungian terms, is the true path to becoming whole.

~ Jason A Solomon

Hashtag Use

This book is an informational resource, not a diagnostic tool or a substitute for professional psychological, medical, or therapeutic support. The hashtags we've selected reflect the core themes explored in these pages and are designed to spark further independent exploration and foster a supportive, informed community online.

For instance, #ShadowWork is a powerful tag that has garnered massive attention on platforms like TikTok and Instagram. It's often associated with personal stories of confronting hidden fears, repressed emotions, and disowned aspects of the self. Through videos, posts, and shared experiences, #ShadowWork opens a dialogue about embracing every facet of our inner lives, even those parts we might prefer to keep hidden.

In tandem, #SelfDiscovery serves as a beacon for those embarking on the journey inward. Social media users employ this tag to share moments of insight, breakthrough revelations, and the ups and downs of finding one's authentic self. It conveys that self-awareness is a gradual, personal exploration, full of diverse experiences and revelations.

Meanwhile, #InnerWork is a reminder of the deliberate, daily practices that support ongoing growth. Whether it's through meditation, journaling, or reflective exercises, this hashtag points to the intentional efforts we make to delve deeper into our inner world and nurture lasting transformation.

Lastly, #HealingJourney encapsulates the long road toward recovery and wholeness. Posts tagged with #HealingJourney illustrate that while setbacks may occur, each step, no matter how small, is significant. They encourage collective empathy and underscore the ongoing process of mending emotional wounds.

Keep in mind, however, that while social media provides a platform for sharing inspiration, the quality and depth of content vary greatly. View these hashtags as signposts pointing toward communities and ideas rather than exhaustive guides. As you navigate your own journey, remember to exercise discernment, and always seek guidance from qualified professionals when addressing issues like emotional trauma, mental health challenges, or therapeutic practices.

You are not broken. You are unfolding. And you are never alone on the path back to yourself.

Contents

14

The shadow is not a punishment. It is a portal. And naming is the first step through.

#ShadowWork #InnerHealing #EmotionalHealing

#TraumaHealing #SelfDiscovery

#HealingJourney #InnerWork

#MentalHealthAwareness #EmotionalWellness

#HealingTrauma #SpiritualHealing

#SubconsciousHealing #RepressedEmotions

#SelfAcceptance #EmbraceYourShadow

#ShadowSelf #IntegrateYourShadow

#HealingFromWithin #SelfAwareness

#EmotionalFreedom #HealingThroughJournaling

#ShadowIntegration #InnerChildHealing

#HealingTheInnerChild #EmotionalResilience

#ConsciousHealing #SelfReflection #LettingGo

#HealingLight #RadicalSelfLove #DeepHealing

#SoulHealing #EnergyHealing

#EmotionalGrowth #MindBodySoul

#SpiritualAwakening #MentalHealthJourney

#TransformYourPain #FromWoundToWisdom

#HealYourPast #HealingMyself

#AwakenYourSoul #PurgeToHeal

#EmotionalAlchemy #FaceYourShadow

#DarkNightOfTheSoul #FeelToHeal

#EmotionsMatter #WoundedHealer

#ReleaseThePain #ShadowWorkTools

#SoulAlchemy #SacredShadow

#HealingEmotions #EmotionalDetox

#HolisticHealing #EmotionalIntegration

#JournalingForHealing

#HealingThroughAwareness

#AwarenessIsHealing #EmotionalDepth

#SubconsciousReprogramming

#SelfHealingTools #EmbraceAllOfYou

#HealingIsNotLinear #ShadowHealing

#HealingCrisis #EmotionalRelease

#HealingDaily #SelfCompassion #InnerAlchemy

#HealingInProgress #BefriendYourShadow

#EmbraceTheDark #WholenessWork

#PsycheHealing #EmotionalTruth

#HealingEnergy #EmotionalCleansing

#SoulGrowth #SpiritHealing #EmotionalSupport

#ShadowWorkJourney #HealingTogether

#FeelToTransform #PurgeAndRenew

Introduction

We often believe that growth is a forward motion, that we must strive, achieve, and become more of what we think we should be. But in truth, real transformation is often backward. It asks us to turn inward and downward, into the forgotten basement of the psyche. There, in the corners we avoid, lives everything we once hid to survive: our anger, our fear, our unmet needs, our unspoken desires, our brilliance that was too loud for someone else's comfort.

This book is about what happens when we stop running from those corners.

Shadow work, a term rooted in the early 20th-century psychological writings of Carl Gustav Jung, refers to the conscious engagement with the unconscious parts of ourselves. These are the aspects that do not align with our self-image or social ideals, so we repress them. They don't disappear. They simply go underground. And what we push into the dark often finds other ways to emerge: in our relationships, our self-talk, our coping mechanisms, and our cycles of self-sabotage.

The shadow is not inherently evil or wrong. It is a container for everything that was not welcomed in us. In many cases, that includes our strength, our boundaries, our intuition, and our capacity to say no. What begins as survival eventually becomes self-denial. And when we live long enough denying ourselves, we become strangers to our inner life.

Today, *shadow work* has resurfaced in popular language, shared widely under hashtags like #HealingJourney, #SelfDiscovery, #InnerWork, and #ShadowIntegration. Yet as with many rising terms in personal development, its meaning is often diluted or romanticized.

This compiled research seeks to restore depth and clarity to the concept. It does not offer a step-by-step method or promise breakthrough results. Instead, it serves as a psychological primer, an educational exploration of what shadow work is, how it functions, and why it matters in the context of your inner world.

You will not find daily affirmations or worksheets in these pages. What you will find is an *informed structure* for thinking critically and compassionately about the parts of yourself you've inherited, absorbed, hidden, or disowned.

You'll learn:

> ➢ How the shadow forms during childhood and how it shapes adult behaviour
> ➢ Why emotions like shame, envy, and rage often point toward disowned parts
> ➢ How the nervous system and relational wounds influence repression
> ➢ What it means to integrate, not eliminate, your darker emotional material
> ➢ How cultural, familial, and generational dynamics shape the collective shadow
> ➢ Why wholeness is not perfection, but conscious contradiction

This resource does not diagnose or prescribe. It invites you to *understand.* And understanding, Jung reminds us, is the beginning of healing, not because it fixes the pain, but because it makes us whole again.

The Unseen Self

What the Shadow Is, Where It Comes From, and Why We All Have One

> *"How can I be substantial if I do not cast a shadow?"*
> ~ *Carl Gustav Jung*

We are taught from an early age how to *be good*. But rarely are we taught how to be whole.

From the moment we learn to speak, we begin shaping a version of ourselves designed to be accepted. We pick up signals from our parents, teachers, peers, and society about what is "right," "good," or "lovable" ~ and we quickly learn what is not. We adjust accordingly, often unconsciously, splitting ourselves into two categories: the parts we show and the parts we hide. Over time, the hidden parts accumulate, forming what Carl Gustav Jung called the shadow.

The shadow is not evil. It is not a personality flaw. It is simply the unseen self ~ the unconscious storehouse of traits, impulses, emotions, and memories that we have exiled from our conscious identity. These may include obvious elements like anger, jealousy, or pride. But often, the shadow contains aspects that are *positive but socially unwelcome* ~ such as assertiveness, sensuality, ambition, or even deep sensitivity.

We bury what makes others uncomfortable. But buried does not mean gone.

The Birth of the Shadow

The shadow begins to form in childhood. In developmental psychology, children learn to navigate the world by seeking safety and connection. When certain behaviours lead to punishment, neglect, or disapproval, the child internalizes the message: *This part of me is not okay.* Rather than risk abandonment, they push those parts into hiding. The psyche creates a split ~ what Jung called the persona (the mask we show the world) and the shadow (what we suppress beneath it).

These early lessons are not always the result of overt trauma. They can stem from subtle messages, cultural values, or even praise that rewards only one version of who we are. A child praised for being quiet may suppress their natural boldness. A boy who's shamed for crying may bury his grief under layers of control or rage. A girl told to "stop showing off" may hide her brilliance behind people-pleasing.

What's important is not the behaviour itself, but what the child learns to *associate with danger or rejection.* And thus begins the lifelong relationship with the shadow.

Suppression Is Not Resolution

When something is repressed, it doesn't disappear ~ it becomes unconscious. It influences our behaviour from the inside out. The more rigidly we cling to our idealized self-image, the more power the shadow gains. It begins to express itself in subtle ways:

- ➤ In overreactions to small triggers
- ➤ In judgment of others who display the qualities we've disowned
- ➤ In compulsions, addictions, and self-sabotage
- ➤ In relationships that reflect our unresolved inner dynamics

Jung famously said, *"Until you make the unconscious conscious, it will direct your life and you will call it fate."* The shadow is the *unacknowledged director* of many of our emotional reactions and repeated life patterns.

The Modern Myth of "Staying Positive"

In today's culture of toxic positivity, the shadow is often misunderstood. Many self-help narratives imply that if you just "focus on the good," you can outgrow your pain. But the parts we repress don't go quietly. They wait. And they surface in moments of vulnerability, conflict, or stress ~ not to destroy us, but to be integrated.

True growth does not mean avoiding your shadow. It means *befriending it.*

It means recognizing that wholeness includes contradiction. That light is meaningful only in relation to darkness. That healing is not about "becoming good" but *becoming real* ~ reclaiming the full spectrum of who you are.

Why This Matters

Shadow work is not about excavating your past for pain's sake. Nor is it about moralizing your hidden traits. It is about clarity ~ about seeing what you could not see before and holding it with compassion. This act alone changes your relationship to self, to others, and to life.

The shadow is not a flaw in your design. It is a result of adaptation. And by making it conscious, you begin the process of returning to psychological wholeness.

This is not a journey of becoming someone new. It is a process of becoming fully you.

The Inner Child & the Protective Psyche

> *"In every adult there lurks a child ~ an eternal child, something that is always becoming, is never completed, and calls for unceasing care, attention, and education."*
> ~ *Carl Gustav Jung*

The shadow does not emerge in adulthood ~ it is *inherited, shaped, and sealed* during the earliest years of our life. To understand how and why we bury aspects of ourselves, we must revisit the inner child, the psychological construct representing the younger self who experienced early emotional, physical, or relational dissonance. Shadow work, then, begins as a kind of inner archaeology.

We do not grow up and leave the past behind. We carry it with us in behavioural adaptations, emotional reactions, and deeply embedded beliefs. We live in adult bodies, speak with adult vocabularies, and wear adult responsibilities ~ but beneath it all are the protective mechanisms we formed in response to the environments of our earliest years. These parts of us are intelligent. They are protective. And often, they are scared.

The Birthplace of Fragmentation

During childhood, the psyche is exquisitely sensitive to approval, connection, and emotional safety. Children interpret praise as permission to exist. They interpret rejection as a sign that something in them must be hidden. These early perceptions don't require overt abuse to be impactful ~ sometimes they arise from subtle emotional neglect, cultural expectations, mis attuned caregiving, or even well-meaning parents who unintentionally pass on unresolved pain.

When a child senses that certain emotions (such as anger or sadness) or traits (such as boldness or emotional sensitivity) are unwelcome, they internalize a core belief: *Something in me is not okay.* To avoid abandonment or disapproval, they split off this part. The result? The beginnings of shadow material.

These early splits are not errors. They are *adaptations.*

Protective Personas: Inner Armor That Stays Too Long

Out of the fragmented self comes the protective psyche ~ a network of inner roles and personas designed to maintain safety and belonging. These roles form what Internal Family Systems (IFS) therapy refers to as *parts* ~ semi-autonomous identities developed to shield the wounded inner child. Common examples include:

  ➢ The Perfectionist – keeps standards high to avoid criticism
  ➢ The Caretaker – over-functions to earn love through service
  ➢ The Rebel – defies rules to avoid vulnerability or control
  ➢ The Peacemaker – avoids conflict to maintain external harmony
  ➢ The Performer – seeks applause to feel temporarily valid
  ➢ The Controller – tries to manage chaos as a substitute for trust

These roles are not pathological. They are brilliant ~ at least in the environment where they were born. The problem arises when these protective strategies harden into permanent identities. What protected us as children often limits us as adults.

We grow older, but the protection stays. The mask becomes our face. And we begin to mistake adaptation for authenticity.

Trauma and the Exiled Self

At the core of the protective psyche lies the exile ~ a part of the self burdened with emotion too overwhelming to face directly. In IFS theory, exiles carry shame, fear, grief, or unmet needs. They are hidden by protector parts that function like gatekeepers, preventing access to emotional overwhelm.

The paradox is this: we cannot become whole by protecting ourselves from what needs healing. The longer the exiled self remains buried, the more power it exerts from the unconscious. Emotional outbursts, conflict avoidance, co-dependency, or chronic over-functioning are not just bad habits ~ they are signals that some part of us is still in hiding.

Shadow work invites us to acknowledge the protectors ~ not to destroy them, but to thank them and gently retire their role. Only then can we approach the exiled inner child not as a problem to be fixed, but as a presence that still longs to be witnessed.

Self-Compassion as Re-Parenting

The practice of self-compassion, often misunderstood as indulgence, is one of the most profound forms of re-integration. To bring shadow material into awareness without attacking it requires the ability to hold *internal contradiction* without collapsing into shame.

Re-parenting is not about recreating your childhood. It's about giving your inner child what they never received:

> ➢ Consistent self-validation
> ➢ Boundaries that create safety
> ➢ Permission to feel

26

Emotional honesty without punishment

When you relate to your hidden parts with curiosity instead of contempt, they begin to soften. The need for the mask diminishes. And your protective psyche, once exhausted from holding up the walls, can finally rest.

Parts, Personas, and the Mask

> *"The persona is that which in reality one is not, but which oneself as well as others think one is."*
> ~ *Carl Gustav Jung*

As children, we created strategies to be accepted. As adults, we call these strategies *personalities*. But beneath every behaviour that earns approval lies a deeper question: *Who am I when I'm not performing?* In this chapter, we explore how our inner psyche develops a constellation of parts and personas, designed not to deceive others but to protect the self. These constructs become the mask ~ what Jung referred to as the *persona* ~ that we wear to survive social reality.

We all have parts. And in healthy individuals, these parts work in cooperation. But when some parts dominate while others remain suppressed, we begin to over-identify with the role we perform, mistaking it for our essence.

The Role of the Persona

Jung defined the persona as a social mask ~ the version of ourselves we present to fit societal expectations. While the persona helps us function (for instance, being polite, composed, or professionally confident), problems arise when we become fused with it.

Consider the person who is always "the strong one." Or the one who is endlessly optimistic. Or always in control. These aren't flaws ~ they are strategies. But when we over-identify with them, we lose access to the fuller emotional spectrum underneath.

What the world sees may be impressive. But the self that lives behind the mask often feels hollow, anxious, or disoriented by quiet moments.

Internal Parts and the Multiplicity of Self

Modern therapeutic models like Internal Family Systems (IFS) describe the mind not as a unified monolith but as a system of *parts* ~ each with its own perspective, emotion, and agenda. These include:

> ➤ Manager parts: keep daily life organized and stable (e.g., achiever, perfectionist)
> ➤ Firefighter parts: react when pain surfaces (e.g., numbing behaviours, anger)

Exiles: carry burdens of trauma, shame, or unmet need

Each part forms to protect the core self from emotional overwhelm or perceived danger. When parts are out of balance ~ when one is dominant and others are suppressed ~ we experience inner conflict or burnout. Shadow work aims not to silence these parts, but to *understand their purpose* and restore internal harmony.

Signs You're Living from a Mask

> ➤ You feel exhausted by constant performance or "holding it together"
> ➤ You find it hard to name your needs or feelings without guilt
> ➤ You over-function in relationships, work, or family dynamics
> ➤ You struggle to rest, receive, or be emotionally vulnerable

➢ You fear being "found out" for not being who others think you are

These are not signs of weakness ~ they're signs that a part of you has been carrying too much for too long.

Removing the Mask ≠ Losing the Self

The fear of removing the mask is understandable. For many, it has been their survival tool. But the purpose of shadow work is not to remove the mask and expose the raw psyche without support ~ it's to *gradually reduce dependency on the mask* by integrating the self behind it.

We ask:

➢ What was this mask protecting me from?
➢ When did it begin to form?

What is the part behind the mask trying to say?

The more we listen, the less we need to control. And as trust develops between our internal parts, we gain access to deeper authenticity.

Wholeness Over Performance

You are not broken because you wear a mask. You are likely very adaptive, socially aware, and emotionally intelligent. But behind that adaptation lives a human who longs to be *real*.

To bring our personas into conscious awareness is to begin walking the bridge between performance and personhood. That bridge is shadow work. And the goal is not to destroy the mask, but to know the self that created it ~ and to choose when and why you wear it.

Understanding Internal Parts & The Mask

The Structure of the Psyche (IFS-Inspired)

Part	Primary Role	Shadow Implication
Persona (Mask)	Social self; what you present to the world	Over-identification leads to disconnection from the real self
Manager Parts	Maintain order and functionality (e.g., perfectionist, planner)	Can suppress emotion and over-control relationships
Firefighter Parts	React to emotional pain with urgency (e.g., bingeing, anger, distraction)	May act out suppressed shadow traits
Exiles	Hold deep wounds and vulnerable emotions (e.g., shame, fear, grief)	Core of many shadow traits; often hidden and disowned
Core Self	Calm, compassionate inner awareness	Becomes more accessible when parts are seen and integrated

31

Common Personas and Their Hidden Drivers

Persona Role	What It Projects	What It Protects
The Achiever	Capability, control	Fear of failure or worthlessness
The Caretaker	Selflessness, loyalty	Fear of abandonment or rejection
The Stoic	Strength, stability	Shame around vulnerability or emotion
The Optimist	Positivity, motivation	Unprocessed grief or suppressed anger
The Rebel	Independence, defiance	Fear of being dominated or invalidated

Reflection Prompts (Optional Box Format in Layout)

- ➢ What persona do I most often perform in public or close relationships?
- ➢ Which part of me feels exhausted, unheard, or unacknowledged?
- ➢ What am I afraid will happen if I stop playing this role?
- ➢ Can I begin to meet the need behind the mask instead of hiding it?

Projections and Triggers

"Everything that irritates us about others can lead us to an understanding of ourselves."
~ *Carl Gustav Jung*

Shadow work is rarely tidy. It doesn't present itself in neat reflections or scheduled breakthroughs. More often, it emerges sideways ~ through frustration, judgment, envy, blame, or unexpected emotional reactions to other people's behaviour. These moments feel external, but they're actually invitations.

They are the psychological mechanism Jung called projection.

To project is to unknowingly assign a disowned part of yourself onto someone else. You don't just see them ~ you see *you*, distorted and displaced. And the part of you that's still unconscious reacts with discomfort, rejection, or even fixation.

Understanding projection is a cornerstone of shadow work. Because what we reject in others often points to what we have buried in ourselves.

What Is Projection?

Psychologically, projection occurs when you unconsciously transfer traits, emotions, or desires you cannot accept in yourself onto someone else. This is not manipulation or gaslighting ~ it's automatic. The ego avoids discomfort by pushing it outside.

- You criticize a friend for being "selfish" when you secretly long to say no to everyone.
- You envy someone's confidence but label it arrogance because you've suppressed your own voice.
- You feel deeply irritated by someone's emotional expression because you were taught yours was too much.

Projection distorts reality. It creates a world where the "problem" always lives in someone else. But the reaction it triggers is a map to your shadow.

Triggers Are Mirrors

Emotional triggers ~ those sudden surges of anger, shame, defensiveness, or discomfort ~ are not flaws in your system. They are evidence of something deeper asking for attention. Most often, a trigger is not about the other person at all. It's about what they've activated in you.

Common triggers include:

- Criticism (real or perceived)
- Authority figures or power imbalances
- People who are emotionally expressive or emotionally distant
- Being ignored, corrected, challenged, or misunderstood
- Displays of confidence, vulnerability, sensuality, or need

Each of these can touch an unhealed wound, an exiled emotion, or a suppressed trait. Instead of interpreting the trigger as a sign of wrongdoing, shadow work asks: *What part of me is being revealed here?*

Envy, Disgust, and Obsession

Signals from the Psyche

Certain emotional responses are often misunderstood but highly revealing:

Envy: You may want what they have ~ or more precisely, what they *allow themselves to have.* Your envy might be pointing to a desire that you've buried out of fear or shame.

Disgust: You might be rejecting in someone else a quality that mirrors an unaccepted part of yourself. The stronger the aversion, the more likely there is projection at play.

Obsession or idealization: Sometimes we don't project the bad ~ we project the good. We elevate others because they embody something we disowned: boldness, freedom, sensuality, brilliance. This creates power imbalances and chronic self-minimization.

Every strong emotional reaction to someone else is an opportunity. You don't have to act on it, indulge it, or suppress it ~ but you *can examine it.* That is the beginning of integration.

What Projection Looks Like in Relationships

Most of us don't fall in love with others ~ we fall in love with our projections of them. Likewise, we don't always fight about facts ~ we fight about perceived threats to our identity.

In partnerships, friendships, family systems, and workplaces, projection creates misunderstanding and co-dependency:

> ➢ We demand others meet needs we haven't even acknowledged in ourselves.
> ➢ We blame others for emotions we're afraid to feel.
> ➢ We fear rejection and then behave in ways that ensure we're rejected.
> ➢ We try to control others to avoid feeling out of control internally.

Shadow work in relationships involves owning your experience. This doesn't mean you excuse harm or bypass accountability. It means you *take back your projection* and ask: *What story am I bringing into this dynamic? What old fear or role is being reactivated?*

The Antidote:
Self-Responsibility and Curiosity

Projection is a survival response, but integration is a conscious one. To interrupt projection, we must pause long enough to examine our reactivity with curiosity instead of certainty.

Try asking yourself:

> ➢ What is this person showing me that I disown in myself?
> ➢ Where have I felt this before?
> ➢ What am I afraid this moment says about *me*?
> ➢ Can I hold this discomfort long enough to hear what it's teaching me?

When we ask these questions sincerely, we begin to peel back layers of misunderstanding. We stop outsourcing blame. We stop turning away from the parts of us that long to be reclaimed.

The goal is not to stop reacting forever ~ it's to relate to our reactions with enough awareness that they no longer control us.

Naming What We've Buried

"Until you make the unconscious conscious, it will direct your life and you will call it fate."
~ Carl Gustav Jung

You cannot integrate what you cannot name. Shadow work often begins with vague discomfort ~ cycles we repeat, emotions that flare, relationships that spiral ~ but without conscious language, the shadow remains shapeless. It lurks beneath awareness, shaping perception and behaviour like a puppet master behind the curtain.

Naming is how we begin to see. Naming breaks the spell.

In this chapter, we move from theory to recognition. We look at the subtle and specific ways the shadow hides ~ not in what we forget, but in what we avoid, distort, and deny. To name what's been buried is to turn on the light in a long-abandoned room. Dust rises, yes. But so does clarity.

Why We Bury Parts of Ourselves

The psyche is not random. It is protective, brilliant, and loyal to its earliest programming. When a trait, emotion, or need was met with punishment, rejection, or neglect, it became dangerous to express.

To survive, we split off the part of us that felt unsafe. We didn't lose it. We buried it.

This buried material becomes the content of the shadow:

➢ Anger in a family that praised silence
➢ Sadness in a culture that shames vulnerability
➢ Creativity in a system that values conformity
➢ Desire in a household that suppressed sensuality
➢ Boundaries in a role that demanded self-sacrifice

The more consistently we disown a part, the more unconscious ~ and therefore more powerful ~ it becomes. Eventually, we forget it was ever there.

The Lies We Live By

Before we can name the shadow, we must confront the *false narratives* we've internalized to keep it hidden. These are the inner lies that protect the split ~ but keep us fragmented.

Common internal lies include:

➢ *"I'm fine."* (When you're not.)
➢ *"I don't care."* (When you deeply do.)
➢ *"That's just who I am."* (When it's actually who you became to survive.)
➢ *"They're the problem."* (When the pain began long before them.)
➢ *"I shouldn't feel this way."* (When your feeling is actually the gateway to truth.)

Each of these lies was adaptive once. They helped you fit in, avoid conflict, or keep the peace. But now, they block access to your emotional reality.

Naming what you've buried means dismantling these protective scripts and being willing to ask: What is more true than this story?

The Language of the Shadow

One of the most effective ways to begin naming shadow material is to listen to your emotional language ~ especially in moments of defensiveness, judgment, and withdrawal. These are clues.

Pay attention to:

- ➤ What adjectives you use to describe people you dislike
- ➤ What qualities in others make you uncomfortable or reactive
- ➤ What compliments are hardest for you to receive
- ➤ What feedback triggers immediate denial or explanation
- ➤ What you fear others might "find out" about you

The emotions behind these patterns ~ shame, fear, rage, guilt ~ are not weaknesses. They are signposts.

Journaling for Clarity

To bring buried material to the surface, structured journaling can serve as a mirror. Here are a few powerful prompts to begin:

- ➤ What parts of myself do I judge, avoid, or minimize?
- ➤ Who or what triggers an outsized emotional response in me? Why?
- ➤ What traits have I admired or envied in others that I believe I "could never be"?
- ➤ What core belief about myself am I most afraid might be true?
- ➤ If no one were watching or judging, what part of myself would I explore or express more freely?

You don't need to answer perfectly. You only need to answer honestly.

The act of writing bypasses the rational mind's defences. It lets the shadow speak in your own language. And the moment something is named, it loses its ability to operate invisibly.

Naming Is Not Shaming

It is essential to approach this process without judgment. The shadow is not a moral flaw. It is a reflection of what was unsafe, unspeakable, or unacceptable *in context*. You did not bury these parts because you were broken ~ you buried them because you were wise. You adapted to survive.

Now you are safe enough to go back and listen.

To name something is not to condemn it. It is to recognize it as part of your story, and to decide ~ consciously ~ what to do with it now. Some parts may no longer serve you. Others may hold power, beauty, and truth that you're finally ready to reclaim.

Visualizing and Dialoguing with the Shadow

> *"The shadow is a moral problem that challenges the whole ego-personality, for no one can become conscious of the shadow without considerable moral effort."*
> ~ *Carl Gustav Jung*

Once you begin to name what's been buried, a natural question arises: *Now what?* Recognizing the shadow is only the beginning. The deeper work lies in developing a conscious relationship with it. Not to control it. Not to fix it. But to know it.

In analytical psychology, Jung emphasized the value of symbolic exploration. The psyche doesn't always speak in linear language ~ it expresses itself through images, dreams, sensation, metaphor, and voice. This is why visualization and internal dialogue are such powerful tools. They let us speak the native language of the unconscious.

This chapter explores how to intentionally engage with shadow material through symbolic interaction. This is not performance or imagination ~ it is relationship building with the parts of you that were long unseen.

Why Visualization Works

Visualization is not fantasy. It is embodied imagination ~ a way to meet aspects of the self in a setting where logic relaxes and meaning can emerge organically. The unconscious mind responds to image, emotion, and metaphor more than rational analysis.

When we visualize the shadow, we give it shape. We give it a voice. We stop treating it as a lurking threat and begin to encounter it as a presence with intelligence, history, and emotional weight.

You are not summoning a demon. You are giving form to a part of yourself that has waited a long time to be heard.

Visualizing Your Shadow

A guided process to meet your shadow in visualization may look like this:

1. Find a quiet space. Sit comfortably and breathe deeply for several minutes.
2. Imagine yourself walking into a symbolic space ~ a cave, a forest, a dimly lit hallway. Let your psyche choose the setting.
3. In the distance, a figure begins to appear. You don't force it. You allow it to take shape. This is the *embodied form* of your shadow.
4. Notice: What does it look like? How old is it? What is its posture, its energy, its expression?
5. Walk closer. Sit beside it. Ask: *What do you want me to know?*
6. Let it speak. Let it show you something. Don't correct it. Don't justify or defend.
7. When the time feels right, thank it. Return to yourself slowly.

Afterward, you may journal what you saw or felt. Often, the first encounter is surprising. The shadow might appear younger than you. It may be angry. It may cry. It may say nothing. But it will speak again if you keep coming back.

Dialogue: Letting the Shadow Speak

You can also begin a dialogue with the shadow using written or spoken language. This technique, similar to Jung's concept of *active imagination*, allows different parts of the psyche to speak to each other directly.

Try this approach:

1. On paper, divide the page in half. On one side, write as yourself. On the other, as your shadow.
2. Begin with a simple question: *Why do you hide from me?* or *What are you afraid I'll do if I see you?*
3. Let the shadow answer without editing or moralizing.
4. Keep the exchange going. Listen. Challenge if needed. But always return to compassion.

This process often reveals core emotional truths, repressed memories, or patterns of protection. You might hear the shadow say:

➢ You left me when we were hurt.
➢ I'm still carrying the anger you pretend isn't there.
➢ I speak in jealousy because you keep silencing my longing.
➢ I don't want to ruin your life ~ I want to be part of it.

These messages are not always pretty. But they are honest. And shadow work is about becoming strong enough to hear the honesty of your own pain.

Meeting Archetypes and Inner Figures

Sometimes the shadow doesn't appear as a younger version of you. It may arrive as an archetype: the abandoned child, the seductress, the tyrant, the addict, the wounded warrior. These symbolic forms are not just internal ~ they are collective. Jung called them *archetypes of the collective unconscious.*

When a shadow figure appears in this way, you may find resonance across your life:

- ➢ Recurring dreams
- ➢ Attraction to certain films or characters
- ➢ Emotional responses to people with similar traits

These encounters point to *core themes* in your psyche. Rather than fighting or fearing these forms, shadow work invites you to explore what they mean to you, what they have protected, and what wisdom they carry.

Compassion, Not Control

It is essential to remember that the purpose of visualizing and dialoguing with the shadow is not to subdue or fix it ~ it is to understand it. You cannot integrate what you refuse to relate to.

Every act of listening disarms shame. Every act of witnessing builds trust. Over time, the shadow no longer needs to sabotage your relationships or hijack your behaviour ~ because it is no longer alone.

And you? You are no longer fragmented. You are becoming whole.

Releasing and Reframing

> *"We cannot change anything unless we accept it. Condemnation does not liberate, it oppresses."*
> ~ *Carl Gustav Jung*

Bringing the shadow into awareness is an act of radical self-respect. But awareness alone is not integration. Once we have named, visualized, and dialogued with our shadow material, we reach the threshold where healing takes a new form ~ through the conscious release of old identities, stories, and frames of meaning.

In this chapter, we explore what it means to let go not of the shadow itself, but of the stories that keep it chained. We explore how to reframe what was once rejected as something that can now be reclaimed.

Letting Go ≠ Erasing

To release something from the shadow does not mean it disappears. Shadow work is not about removal ~ it's about *recalibration*. You're not erasing the part; you're changing your relationship to it.

When we cling to old roles (the fixer, the caretaker, the rebel) or to narratives forged in trauma ("I'm too much," "My needs don't matter"), we continue to centre our life around survival instead of expansion. These roles once kept us safe, but now they confine us.

Letting go, in this context, means retiring protective scripts that no longer serve your growth. It means stepping out of the old frame and asking: *Who am I without this pattern?*

That question can feel terrifying. It can also be the beginning of freedom.

What We Tend to Hold on To

The things we hold most tightly are often rooted in past pain. For example:

1. Control to avoid chaos
2. Self-reliance to avoid disappointment
3. Silence to avoid conflict
4. Anger to avoid grief
5. Achievement to avoid feelings of worthlessness

These patterns don't persist because we're weak. They persist because they once worked. Shadow work allows us to thank them ~ and then to release the contract.

Ask yourself:

➤ What identity did I form to be accepted or safe?
➤ What am I afraid will happen if I stop living that role?
➤ What part of me is still carrying the burden of "never again"?
➤ Release begins with acknowledgment. It continues with trust.

47

Ritual as Releasing Ceremony

Letting go is a psychological shift ~ but for many, it also requires symbolic action. Rituals offer a concrete way to mark the death of an old story. You may wish to try:

1. Burning a letter to your younger self or an internal part, expressing what you no longer carry
2. Tearing up old narratives you've written out (e.g., "I am never enough")
3. Creating a goodbye list of roles, relationships, or beliefs you are ready to retire
4. Using water, breath, or sound to symbolize cleansing and reset

The point is not the ritual itself ~ it's what the act represents: a moment of conscious surrender.

Reframing: Turning Shadow Into Source

Once released, shadow traits can be reframed ~ not as flaws, but as forms of *potential power*. What you once disowned may now become part of your emotional vocabulary.

Examples of reframing:

➢ "I'm too sensitive" → "My sensitivity is emotional intelligence."
➢ "I'm too angry" → "My anger protects my boundaries."
➢ "I'm selfish" → "I have a right to prioritize my well-being."
➢ "I'm broken" → "I adapted to pain and survived."
➢ "I'm controlling" → "I once had no control, and I'm learning to feel safe again."

Reframing is not denial. It's the integration of shadow traits into a broader, more compassionate understanding of the self. We do not heal by rejecting our darkness ~ we heal by witnessing it with new eyes.

The Grief of Shedding the Old Self

Every act of release comes with grief. Even when we let go of something harmful, we are still letting go of something familiar. The old roles may have limited you, but they were your companions. Grieve them. Thank them. And don't rush the space they leave behind.

Grief is a sign of transition. It tells you that something within you has shifted form. The shadow is not gone ~ but it is no longer your enemy. And in the quiet after the release, something new begins to grow.

You.

Emotional Reactivity and the Body

> *"The pendulum of the mind oscillates between sense and nonsense, not between right and wrong."*
> ~ *Carl Gustav Jung*

We like to think of shadow work as a mental process ~ ideas we analyse, patterns we observe, thoughts we reframe. But in truth, the shadow also lives in the body. It pulses through your nervous system. It tenses in your jaw. It floods your chest during conflict. The body carries what the mind cannot name. And it remembers everything.

This chapter explores the somatic dimension of shadow work ~ how emotional reactivity is not just a psychological pattern, but a physical signal of unresolved material surfacing. To ignore the body is to ignore the earliest language of the shadow.

Why the Body Reacts Before the Mind Understands

When we feel emotionally "hijacked," it often seems irrational. We react suddenly, maybe even disproportionately, to what seems like a small trigger. But what's happening is deeply logical from the body's point of view.

Our nervous system is designed to protect us. When it senses danger ~ real or perceived ~ it activates a survival response: fight, flight, freeze, or fawn. The problem is, unresolved shadow material confuses the body. It associates present-day discomfort with past trauma. You're not just reacting to *this* moment ~ you're reacting to *that* one.

- ➤ That raised voice? It's your father's rage.
- ➤ That criticism? It's your caregiver's judgment.
- ➤ That silence? It's the neglect you never processed.

The shadow is not only psychological ~ it is neurological. And reactivity is its way of speaking through your cells.

Common Somatic Shadow Signals

Your body often knows you're triggered before your mind does. Watch for signals like:

- ➤ Tight chest or throat
- ➤ Jaw clenching, teeth grinding
- ➤ Shallow breath, sighing, or breath-holding
- ➤ Stomach tension or nausea
- ➤ Urge to leave, fix, explain, or shut down
- ➤ Sudden fatigue, brain fog, or numbness

These symptoms are not signs of weakness. They are invitations. Your body is asking you to pause, listen, and attend to something deeper.

From Emotional Reactivity to Embodied Awareness

The goal is not to avoid triggers forever. The goal is to notice and stay present long enough to gain awareness without collapsing into reaction. This requires practice, not perfection.

A few methods include:

Body scanning: Silently scan your body from head to toe. Name what you feel without judging it. (e.g., "tight chest," "heat in belly," "numb hands.")

Breath awareness: Use slow, conscious breathing to calm your nervous system. Inhale for 4 counts, exhale for 6. This down-regulates the fight/flight response.

Somatic journaling: Write from the body's perspective. Ask, "What does this part of me remember?" or "What emotion lives in this tension?"

Movement and release: Shake, stretch, or move gently to help the body process stuck energy. Trauma and shadow often freeze us ~ movement is medicine.

What Happens When We Ignore the Body

If we intellectualize shadow work without involving the body, we risk staying in analysis without transformation. We may be able to name our patterns, but still feel powerless to change them. That's because the shadow doesn't live only in thoughts. It lives in reflexes, patterns, and stored energy.

Ignoring the body means:

- ➤ Suppressed rage gets funnelled into chronic illness or anxiety
- ➤ Unprocessed grief turns into emotional numbness
- ➤ Unexpressed fear surfaces in micro-aggressions or withdrawal
- ➤ Repressed shame appears as perfectionism or people-pleasing

Your body holds the emotional residue of what your mind tried to forget. But it's also your greatest ally in integration ~ if you're willing to listen.

Reclaiming Safety in the Self

Shadow work through the body is not about "getting over" triggers. It's about becoming less afraid of your internal states. It's about staying with discomfort long enough to find meaning inside it.

Every time you feel something rise ~ shame, fear, anger, sadness ~ you have a choice. You can override it. Or you can say: *This belongs. I'm listening.*

And when you listen, the body begins to release what it once held in silence.

That release is not just emotional. It is liberation.

Relational Shadows

> *"Everything that irritates us about others can lead us to an understanding of ourselves."*
> ~ *Carl Gustav Jung*

It's easy to think that shadow work is a solitary task ~ a quiet journey inward, removed from the noise of the outside world. But the truth is, the fastest way to encounter your shadow is in relationships. That's where the hidden parts surface. That's where projections take shape. That's where our emotional reflexes ~ blame, defensiveness, abandonment, control ~ show us what we haven't integrated.

We are never more exposed than when we are trying to connect.

Relationships become mirrors ~ not because others are the same as us, but because they reflect back the unhealed, unseen, or exiled parts of our emotional world. Romantic partners, family members, colleagues, even strangers online can activate dormant material we thought we had already dealt with. And yet ~ it's not a failure. It's an invitation.

Why the Shadow Shows Up in Relationships

Relationships are built on attachment, and attachment is shaped by our earliest emotional experiences. When we bond with others, our nervous system seeks familiarity. That often includes not only love and affection ~ but also unmet needs, unresolved pain, and old survival strategies.

1. If love felt inconsistent, you may chase emotional availability in people who withhold it.
2. If anger was punished, you may suppress conflict until it explodes.
3. If care was conditional, you may over-function or people-please to earn worth.
4. If you were told you were "too much," you may attract people who emotionally withdraw.

These patterns aren't flaws ~ they're *echoes*. The shadow surfaces in relationships because relationship is where the wound began.

Common Relational Shadow Patterns

Projection: Assigning your disowned traits to the other person (e.g., "You're always angry," when you suppress your own anger).

Idealization: Elevating others to avoid facing your own power or capacity (e.g., "They're so confident; I could never be like that.")

Co-dependency: Making yourself responsible for another person's feelings while abandoning your own.

Control: Micromanaging others' behaviour to soothe your own insecurity or fear of loss.

Abandonment cycles: Pushing people away emotionally before they can leave you.

These dynamics don't mean the relationship is doomed. But they do mean that shadow material is present and asking to be acknowledged ~ not projected, blamed, or acted out.

How the Shadow Uses Intimacy to Speak

Relationships ~ especially romantic or familial ones ~ create emotional intimacy, and intimacy is the most fertile ground for the shadow. That's why your partner, sibling, or child can "trigger you" more than anyone else. It's not just because of who they are ~ it's because of who they awaken inside you.

For example:

➢ When your partner forgets something important, it reawakens a buried feeling of invisibility from childhood.
➢ When your friend cancels plans, it triggers the wound of being left out or unimportant.
➢ When your sibling criticizes you, it reactivates the belief that you're never good enough.

The emotional volume of these moments is often disproportionate to the event itself. That's how you know it's not just the present ~ it's the past trying to be heard.

From Reaction to Reflection

Shadow work in relationships doesn't mean staying silent or tolerating harm. It means owning your emotional content ~ so that communication becomes conscious, not compulsive.

Try asking:

> ➢ What part of me is reacting right now?
> ➢ What memory or feeling does this situation stir in me?
> ➢ Am I asking this person to heal something I haven't acknowledged in myself?
> ➢ What am I afraid will happen if I express what I really feel or need?

These questions bring you back to *you* ~ not to remove others' accountability, but to reclaim your own.

Healing in Connection

We are wounded in relationship. But we also heal in relationship. When shadow work is done relationally ~ with mutual respect, boundaries, and emotional maturity ~ it can deepen connection rather than threaten it.

Practices that support relational shadow integration include:

1. **Conscious communication:** Using "I" statements and owning projections.
2. **Repair rituals:** Coming back after conflict to acknowledge what surfaced internally.
3. **Safe witnessing:** Letting others hold space for your vulnerability without fixing or advising.
4. **Therapeutic support:** Working through attachment wounds with professional guidance.

The goal is not to become invulnerable or untriggered. The goal is to become self-aware enough to know when the shadow is speaking ~ and to choose a response rooted in truth rather than protection.

Cultural and Ancestral Inheritance

"It is not I who create myself, rather I happen to myself."
~ *Carl Gustav Jung*

Not all shadow material originates from personal experience. Some of it is passed down ~ quietly, unconsciously ~ through generations, cultures, and systems we did not choose. Before we are shaped by our own choices, we are shaped by our families, our history, and our inherited beliefs about what it means to be human.

In this chapter, we explore the collective and ancestral shadow ~ those aspects of ourselves that were not just buried in childhood, but embedded in the cultural air we breathed. This form of shadow is often more subtle, more systemic, and more difficult to detect ~ because it doesn't feel like an individual wound. It feels like *reality*.

But it's not. It's conditioning.

And shadow work is incomplete without confronting what we've unconsciously inherited.

The Collective Shadow

Carl Jung believed that just as individuals have shadows, so too do collectives: families, communities, institutions, nations. These shared shadows form when entire groups reject certain aspects of human experience in favour of dominance, control, or cultural ideals.

Examples of collective shadow include:

 ➢ Cultures that glorify independence while shaming emotional need
 ➢ Generations that praise stoicism but suppress vulnerability
 ➢ Communities that uphold religious purity while silencing sexuality
 ➢ Societies that reward performance while stigmatizing rest, softness, or slowness

When these cultural shadows go unnamed, they are passed down through shame, silence, or projection. A boy who cries becomes "weak." A woman who speaks up becomes "difficult." A person who struggles is labelled "lazy." These judgments aren't personal ~ they're inherited.

Shadow work at the cultural level asks us: Whose voice are you still obeying?

The Ancestral Shadow

Some of what lives in your shadow didn't begin with you. Intergenerational trauma refers to patterns, emotions, and coping strategies passed from one generation to the next ~ often unconsciously. This includes:

1. Fear-based parenting
2. Secrets or shame around identity, race, gender, or origin
3. Silence about grief, abuse, or historical injustice

4. Repetition of survival behaviours (e.g., hoarding, control, self-denial)
5. Deep loyalty to suffering as a family legacy

Ancestral shadow material is particularly complex because it often exists without language. It may show up as:

1. A heaviness you can't explain
2. Guilt for outgrowing your family's limitations
3. Resistance to ease or joy
4. Chronic over-responsibility for others' pain

You may carry emotions that were never yours to begin with. Shadow work gives you the framework to say: This lives in me, but it may not originate from me.

Uncovering Inherited Beliefs

To bring collective or ancestral shadow into consciousness, ask yourself:

➤ What was I taught was "not okay" in my culture or family system?
➤ What identities or traits were unsafe to express?
➤ What emotional responses were punished, ignored, or mocked?
➤ What roles did people have to play to feel loved or safe?
➤ What patterns keep repeating, even when I try to change?

You're not just excavating your own history. You're uncovering the emotional DNA of the people who came before you ~ and choosing what you no longer need to carry.

Respect Without Repetition

Doing ancestral shadow work does not mean blaming your parents, your lineage, or your community. It means becoming conscious of what was unconscious ~ and choosing not to pass it forward.

We can honor our ancestors without repeating their wounds. We can respect our upbringing without letting it dictate our future. And we can stay connected to our roots while growing beyond their limitations.

Releasing the ancestral shadow is not betrayal. It is evolution.

Healing in the Collective Field

Just as wounds can be passed on, so can healing. The more consciously we examine the systems we live in ~ the more we name what was hidden, speak what was silenced, and feel what was forbidden ~ the more we create space for collective integration.

Shadow work is not only personal. It is political. It is ancestral. It is cultural.

And the more of it we do together, the less we need to exile.

61

What Integration Really Means

> *"Wholeness is not achieved by cutting off a portion of one's being, but by integration of the contraries."*
> ~ *Carl Gustav Jung*

Shadow work is not about perfection. It's not about becoming pure, healed, or emotionally untouchable. If that were the goal, it would only reinforce the same division that created the shadow in the first place. Real shadow work ~ at its depth ~ is the process of integration.

But what does integration actually mean?

- ➢ Not fixing. Not purging.
- ➢ Not transcending.
- ➢ Integration means inclusion.

It means making room in your identity for the parts of you that were once hidden, feared, or misunderstood. Integration is the opposite of disowning. It's not a single moment of healing ~ it's a lifelong dialogue with the full spectrum of your humanity.

Wholeness Over Cleansing

Modern self-help culture often promotes the illusion that inner peace comes from removing anything "toxic" inside of us. But you cannot become whole by cutting away what you don't like.

You become whole by becoming familiar with *all of you* ~ especially the parts that still feel raw, reactive, or unfinished.

Integration is not spiritual hygiene. It's emotional maturity.

It looks like:

➢ Knowing your anger and not being ruled by it
➢ Naming your shame without collapsing into it
➢ Seeing your jealousy as a signal, not a sin
➢ Understanding your fear without letting it make your choices

You can feel these things without becoming them. That is the heart of integration.

Signs of Integration in Daily Life

Integration is quiet. It shows up in the smallest of moments:

➢ You pause before reacting and ask yourself what's really going on
➢ You express a boundary without guilt
➢ You notice a trigger, but stay grounded instead of spiralling
➢ You allow yourself to feel sadness without fixing it
➢ You hold multiple truths about yourself without needing to be either/or

These are not achievements ~ they are indicators of inner harmony. You are no longer at war with your own emotions. You're in conversation with them.

Making Room for Contradiction

One of the deepest signs of integration is the ability to hold opposites without demanding resolution. You begin to accept paradox as part of the human experience:

1. I can be independent and still long for closeness
2. I can feel angry and still love you
3. I can be afraid and still take action
4. I can carry grief and still experience joy
5. I can be healing and still have hard days

Shadow work teaches us that maturity is not about being consistent ~ it's about being honest. And honesty requires the courage to stop labelling some parts of ourselves as wrong.

Internal Balance, Not Internal Silence

People often think that once they "do the work," their inner world will become silent. That's not integration ~ that's repression in disguise.

The integrated self doesn't silence the shadow ~ it listens to it. And in listening, it learns how to lead.

You begin to know:

➤ Which part of you is speaking in a given moment
➤ What emotion is present, and what it's asking for
➤ When to sit with discomfort, and when to act
➤ How to protect yourself without punishing others
➤ How to feel deeply without being consumed

Integration is not the absence of inner complexity. It is the presence of conscious leadership within your own psyche.

Wholeness Is Not a Destination

There is no arrival point in shadow work. No final state of being "fully integrated." That idea itself is a projection of perfectionism. Instead, integration is cyclical. As you grow, new aspects of your shadow will reveal themselves. Not because you've failed ~ but because you've become safe enough to see more clearly.

Each new layer of self-awareness deepens your compassion. Each return to the shadow is less fearful than the last.

And slowly, the parts of you that once fought each other begin to speak the same language. That language is not judgment.

It's acceptance.

The Continuum of Integration

> *"One does not become enlightened by imagining figures of light, but by making the darkness conscious."*
> ~ *Carl Gustav Jung*

Shadow work does not end. That's not a flaw in the process; it's the nature of being human.

We are not puzzles to be solved, but ecosystems to be witnessed, and like any living system, our internal world is always evolving. The point of this work is not to "finish." The point is to participate consciously in your own becoming.

This chapter is not a conclusion. It's a compass. A reminder that integration is not a destination but a continuum ~ a rhythm of noticing, naming, feeling, reframing, releasing, and returning.

You Will Loop Back

You will revisit old wounds, even after you've done "the work." You will get triggered by something you thought you had healed. This is not regression. This is *deepening.*

Each cycle reveals a new layer:

- ➤ A more nuanced emotion
- ➤ A quieter form of resistance
- ➤ A subtler self-betrayal

➢ A softer, more truthful boundary
➢ The loop is not proof you're stuck. It's proof you're still open.

Indicators You're on the Path

➢ You may not always feel transformed. But you might notice:
➢ You pause instead of reacting
➢ You feel your feelings, then choose your response
➢ You recognize projections and reclaim them
➢ You set boundaries without hardening your heart
➢ You let others be flawed without collapsing

These are signs of integration. Not because you are invulnerable, but because you are in right relationship with yourself.

When the Work Feels Heavy

There will be seasons where you'll want to stop. Where growth feels exhausting and emotional honesty feels like too much. In those moments:

➢ Rest.
➢ Re-anchor in joy, beauty, and embodiment.
➢ Stop diagnosing yourself and start *living*.

Let the shadow sit quietly in the background while you take up space in the light.

Integration honors both ends of the spectrum: the healing *and* the living. The descent *and* the dance.

Let It Be Lived, Not Just Studied

This book is not your answer. It's a reflection. The real work begins when you look into your own life and see what's asking to be loved.

> ➤ You don't need to master this process.
> ➤ You need only stay in relationship with it.

With curiosity.

> With courage.

> > With compassion.

The Final Reframe

You were never broken. You were never too much. You were never the wound. You are the space that holds the healing. You are the one who chose to look within. You are the consciousness that turns pain into presence. This is the continuum. This is the work. This is the becoming.

And it's already unfolding through you.

Acknowledgments

No one walks through the shadow alone. This book is born from conversations, reflections, mentors, and unseen hands who have shaped my path.

To the seekers, the sceptics, the overthinkers, and the feelers ~ thank you. To the therapists, thinkers, teachers, and friends who showed me there was more to the story than the surface ~ I am deeply grateful.

To Carl Gustav Jung ~ whose language for the unconscious continues to echo through generations. And to everyone who has ever turned inward with trembling courage and emerged more whole ~ this is for you.

Notes

This book integrates a range of psychological frameworks and language, including:

➤ Carl Gustav Jung's concepts of the *shadow*, *persona*, and *individuation*
➤ Internal Family Systems (IFS) model by Dr. Richard Schwartz
➤ Somatic psychology principles grounded in body-based trauma healing
➤ Attachment theory as developed by Bowlby and Ainsworth
➤ Reflections on projection, repression, and emotional integration

This book is not intended as a therapeutic or diagnostic tool. It is a non-clinical information resource written to illuminate, not prescribe.

Recommended Resources

If you wish to continue your exploration, the following resources offer depth and guidance:

Books & Authors:

> - *Man and His Symbols* ~ Carl Gustav Jung
> - *The Body Keeps the Score* ~ Bessel van der Kolk
> - *No Bad Parts* ~ Richard C. Schwartz
> - Women Who Run With the Wolves ~ Clarissa Pinkola Estés
> - Radical Acceptance ~ Tara Brach
> - The Drama of the Gifted Child ~ Alice Miller
> - Podcasts & Media:
> - The Holistic Psychologist (Dr. Nicole LePera)
> - Therapy Chat
> - On Being with Krista Tippett

Practices to Explore:

> - Somatic experiencing
> - Parts work (IFS)
> - Shadow journaling
> - Guided inner child meditation
> - Breathwork and nervous system regulation

Index of Key Terms

Ancestral Shadow

Refers to the emotional patterns, belief systems, and survival strategies inherited from previous generations. These often live beneath conscious awareness, subtly shaping our identities and relationships.

Attachment Theory

A foundational psychological model that explains how early bonds with caregivers influence emotional regulation, intimacy, and trust throughout life.

Co-dependency

A relational pattern where individuals prioritize the needs, emotions, or validation of others at the expense of their own well-being ~ often in an attempt to maintain control or connection.

Collective Shadow

The unconscious traits or emotions that entire groups, cultures, or societies repress in favour of dominant ideals, leading to widespread projection and systemic dysfunction.

Core Self

The calm, centred presence within ~ the part of the psyche that embodies compassion, clarity, and curiosity. Often obscured by protective or wounded parts but never lost.

Ego Death

The dissolution of an outdated or protective identity, often occurring during a major psychological or spiritual shift. It marks the release of who we thought we had to be.

Emotional Regulation

The capacity to navigate, manage, and respond to emotional experiences in a conscious and adaptive way rather than through reactivity or suppression.

Exiles (IFS)

In Internal Family Systems (IFS) theory, these are the wounded inner parts that carry the pain, shame, or unmet needs of the past and are often pushed away for protection.

Firefighter

Parts Also from IFS, these reactive parts rush in to distract from emotional pain ~ often through addiction, avoidance, anger, or hyper-productivity.

Integration

The conscious inclusion of previously exiled or disowned parts of ourselves into our whole identity. True integration honors complexity rather than seeking purity.

Internal Family Systems (IFS)

A therapeutic model that views the psyche as composed of multiple inner "parts," each with its own voice, story, and protective strategy. Healing occurs through inner dialogue and self-leadership.

Persona

A term from Jungian psychology referring to the social mask we wear ~ the identity shaped to gain approval or protection in our environment.

Projection

The act of attributing your own suppressed traits, fears, or desires to another person. It is a key mechanism of the shadow and often disrupts relationships.

Rebirth

The emergence of a truer, freer self after the collapse of false roles, outdated defences, or inherited identities. Not a single moment but an unfolding process of self-recognition.

Relational Shadow

Aspects of the shadow that surface specifically within intimate, familial, or social relationships ~ often as triggers, roles, or unresolved attachment patterns.

Self-Discovery

The journey of becoming aware of your inner truths, values, and contradictions. Self-discovery is not linear; it is a cyclical process of returning to yourself more consciously.

Shadow

The parts of ourselves we repress, deny, or disown ~ whether due to trauma, culture, or conditioning. The shadow includes both "negative" traits and suppressed strengths.

Shadow Integration

The act of acknowledging and welcoming the shadow into your conscious identity. Integration allows for balance, self-trust, and emotional wholeness.

Somatic Work

Body-centred practices used to regulate the nervous system, process trauma, and reconnect with emotional experiences through physical awareness.

Triggers

Events, behaviours, or sensations that reactivate unresolved emotional content, often rooted in past experiences or unmet needs.

Timeline of Shadow Work

Early 1900s

Freud and the Unconscious

Sigmund Freud introduces the foundational concepts of the unconscious mind, repression, and the idea that much of human behaviour is driven by hidden desires and internal conflicts. His structural model of the psyche ~ id, ego, and superego ~ sets the stage for deeper exploration of what lies beneath our conscious identity.

Freud's legacy paved the way for later thinkers to question what gets pushed into the "dark" when we strive to appear socially acceptable. Although Freud didn't use the term "shadow," his notion of repression closely mirrors the early framing of psychological splitting and internal conflict that would become central to shadow work.

1910s–1930s

Carl Gustav Jung & the Birth of the Shadow

Carl Jung breaks from Freud and proposes a richer vision of the psyche, introducing the "shadow" as a key archetype in the collective unconscious. He describes the shadow as everything within us that we reject, disown, or are unaware of ~ qualities that are incompatible with the ego's self-image.

Jung's concept of individuation ~ the journey toward psychological wholeness ~ relies on recognizing, engaging with, and ultimately integrating the shadow. He argued that true growth requires confronting these darker aspects, not suppressing them. This revolutionary insight remains the backbone of all shadow work frameworks today.

1950s–1970s

Humanistic Psychology & Expanded Self-Inquiry

Humanistic psychology emerges as a response to both psychoanalysis and behaviourism, emphasizing empathy, authenticity, and the drive toward self-actualization. Carl Rogers introduces "unconditional positive regard" as a radical approach to personal development, promoting non-judgmental acceptance of all parts of the self.

Though less focused on unconscious drives, humanistic thinkers implicitly acknowledged the shadow by encouraging emotional honesty, self-exploration, and confronting the "oughts" of societal conditioning. This period broadened the conversation, moving healing from the therapist's office into the realm of personal exploration.

1970s–1990s

Depth Psychology and Somatic Integration

Jungian successors like James Hillman and Marion Woodman reframe the shadow as part of an ongoing mythic narrative rather than a pathology. They introduce symbolic, poetic, and feminine perspectives on the psyche, challenging linear or clinical views of healing. Hillman in particular emphasized the "soul" of symptoms rather than simply trying to fix them.

Meanwhile, pioneers like Peter Levine and Pat Ogden begin developing somatic therapies that view trauma as stored in the body. This expanded the idea of the shadow from purely mental concepts to embodied experience, allowing a more complete engagement with unconscious material through movement, sensation, and nervous system regulation.

1990s–2000s

Internal Family Systems (IFS)

Dr. Richard Schwartz develops IFS, a model that views the psyche as a system of parts ~ each with its own role, history, and emotional tone. Parts may include exiles (wounded aspects), managers (preventative), and firefighters (emergency responders). The "Self," a calm and compassionate presence, leads the system.

IFS shares striking similarities with shadow work, particularly in the way it honors all parts as valuable ~ even those we would typically repress. Instead of demonizing the shadow, IFS offers a method to befriend it. This marks a shift from confrontation to cooperation and has become increasingly popular in both therapy and coaching.

2010s–Present

Trauma-Informed & Cultural Perspectives

In the last decade, shadow work has migrated from academia and therapy rooms into social discourse, spiritual platforms, and digital spaces. Influencers, psychologists, and somatic practitioners emphasize the link between unresolved trauma and shadow dynamics. Gabor Maté's work on childhood trauma and addiction, for instance, highlights the compassionate view of the wounded inner self.

This era also sees greater acknowledgment of systemic shadows: racism, ableism, generational trauma, and cultural suppression. Shadow work is no longer solely about the individual ~ it becomes relational, political, and collective. New models blend ancient wisdom, neuroscience, and intersectional justice, inviting a deeper and more inclusive form of inner inquiry.

Glossary
Psychological Terms

Ancestral Shadow

The unconscious emotional patterns, fears, or coping strategies passed down through generations. These are often absorbed through family systems, not as direct teachings, but as unspoken survival codes embedded in behaviour, silence, or belief.

Many people carry guilt, scarcity, shame, or fear that originated in historical trauma ~ wars, poverty, displacement ~ that were never emotionally resolved by their ancestors. Shadow work invites us to examine whether we're living from old scripts that no longer match our reality, helping us break inherited cycles with awareness and compassion.

Attachment Theory

Developed by John Bowlby and expanded by Mary Ainsworth, this theory explains how early relationships ~ especially with primary caregivers ~ shape the way we relate to others and to ourselves throughout life.

In shadow work, insecure attachment patterns can reveal shadow dynamics: the avoidant who suppresses need, the anxious who over-focuses on others, or the disorganized who swings between extremes. Recognizing attachment wounds can unlock some of the deepest shadow patterns driving adult relationships.

Co-dependency

A behaviour pattern where a person focuses excessively on the needs of others, often losing touch with their own emotional boundaries. Common in trauma-impacted families, co-dependency is often driven by a fear of abandonment, conflict, or unworthiness.

Co-dependency can be a shadow mask: a socially rewarded way to hide deeper wounds of rejection or invisibility. Healing involves learning self-responsibility, emotional honesty, and the ability to disappoint others without collapsing your self-worth.

Collective Shadow

These are the values, traits, or impulses a group or culture represses to maintain order or identity. For example, Western cultures may disown emotional vulnerability, while others repress sexuality, dissent, or even joy.

When a collective shadow is denied, it tends to manifest as social injustice, cultural scapegoating, or group polarization. Recognizing the collective shadow invites us to reclaim our participation in these dynamics ~ without shame, but with agency.

Core Self

The internal, unchanging centre of awareness that remains calm, curious, and compassionate ~ even when other parts are triggered or afraid. In IFS and Jungian frameworks, the Core Self is not a mask, but a witness.

The more we operate from this Self, the more integrated we become. Shadow work doesn't aim to destroy reactive parts ~ it aims to bring them into conscious relationship with the Core Self, where they can be seen, soothed, and reintegrated.

81

Ego Death

A profound psychological shift in which an identity that once provided safety, belonging, or power dissolves. This can feel disorienting, as if you're losing yourself ~ when in truth, you are shedding a self that was never fully you.

Ego death often precedes rebirth. It may be triggered by trauma, illness, spiritual awakening, or the cumulative weight of living out of alignment. It's not the death of the ego altogether ~ it's the release of its control.

Emotional Regulation

The ability to manage, express, and respond to emotions in a balanced way. This doesn't mean avoiding emotion ~ it means allowing emotional waves without drowning or numbing out.

Emotional regulation is foundational to shadow integration. Without it, we risk collapsing into shame or exploding in defence. With it, we gain the bandwidth to sit with discomfort long enough to heal.

Exiles (IFS)

These are the wounded parts of the psyche that carry the most pain ~ often locked away after trauma or emotional overwhelm. They hold unmet needs, shame, grief, or terror, and are often protected by other "parts" who prevent access.

Shadow work often involves identifying and eventually comforting these exiles. Reintegrating them helps restore energy, creativity, and emotional openness once blocked by defence.

Firefighter Parts (IFS)

Reactive parts of the psyche that step in quickly when an exile is close to surfacing. They "put out the fire" by numbing, distracting, or exploding ~ through food, addiction, rage, perfectionism, etc.

These behaviours are often misunderstood as character flaws. Shadow work reframes them as trauma responses attempts to protect the system from pain it once couldn't bear.

Integration

The process of accepting and including previously repressed or fragmented parts of the self into conscious identity. Integration is not about fixing or erasing wounds ~ it's about holding paradox.

A person who is integrated does not need to appear perfect. They can name their shadow, sit with discomfort, and choose from a place of awareness rather than reaction. Integration is the soft power of wholeness.

Internal Family Systems (IFS)

A therapeutic framework developed by Richard C. Schwartz that views the psyche as an internal system of "parts," each playing a role in response to past experience.

IFS is one of the most intuitive and compassionate methods of shadow integration. It allows us to view our internal conflict not as dysfunction, but as a system doing its best to protect the whole.

Persona

A concept from Jung, the persona is the social mask we wear to navigate the expectations of others. It's not inherently fake ~ but it becomes problematic when mistaken for the whole self.

Shadow work helps you recognize when you're over-identified with your persona and neglecting other authentic aspects of yourself. Dismantling the persona doesn't mean losing your identity ~ it means expanding it.

Projection

The unconscious act of attributing one's own disowned feelings or traits onto someone else. Often, what we can't tolerate in ourselves, we claim to see in others ~ judgment, envy, weakness, etc.

Projection is a key entry point into shadow awareness. When a reaction feels disproportionate or repetitive, it's often a sign we're meeting our own shadow in the mirror of another.

Rebirth

The experience of emerging into a more truthful, aligned version of self ~ usually after a period of breakdown, confusion, or transformation.

Rebirth is rarely tidy. It can feel like grief, loss, and liberation all at once. It signifies not becoming someone new, but returning to someone real ~ someone you had to hide to survive.

Relational Shadow

Shadow aspects that specifically surface in relationships, often with those closest to us. These may include unmet needs for control, safety, or recognition.

In this space, we unconsciously recreate family dynamics, attachment wounds, or childhood roles. Doing shadow work relationally means identifying these patterns, taking responsibility, and practicing vulnerability over projection.

Self-Discovery

The ongoing journey of uncovering your inner truths, contradictions, wounds, and values. Self-discovery is cyclical, not linear, and often deepens through challenge, reflection, and emotional honesty.

The more you discover, the more you come into relationship with your full self ~ including the parts you were taught to hide. Shadow work is not separate from self-discovery; it is a deep expression of it.

Shadow

The psychological concept describing the unconscious or denied aspects of self. This includes what we repress because it's "unacceptable," as well as what we fail to recognize because it feels too powerful, sensitive, or unfamiliar.

Shadow doesn't mean evil. It means unseen. It can include shame, rage, brilliance, or sensitivity ~ whatever didn't fit the script you were told to follow.

Shadow Integration

The process of consciously meeting, reclaiming, and befriending the shadow. Integration means turning toward the parts of ourselves we once avoided, feared, or projected onto others.

It's not about glorifying the dark. It's about holding the dark and the light together with curiosity and care. It's how we become less reactive and more real.

Somatic Work

Body-based approaches to trauma healing and emotional regulation. Rather than analysing emotions cognitively, somatic work helps process them through movement, breath, and bodily awareness.

In shadow work, somatic tools help release stored trauma that words cannot reach. When the body is included, the healing deepens ~ because the body remembers what the mind forgets.

Triggers

Emotional flashpoints that activate unresolved wounds or unconscious beliefs. They are not just reactions to the present ~ they are echoes of past experiences.

Shadow work reframes triggers as invitations to deeper self-awareness. They aren't signs of failure; they are signposts pointing to parts of us still waiting to be seen.

Thematic Case Snapshots

Snapshot 1: The Performer Who Couldn't Rest

Theme: Persona Fatigue + Emotional Suppression
(#InnerWork #SelfAwareness)

Carla was known as the "go-to" person at work ~ hyper-competent, always smiling, never missing a deadline. She wore her reliability like armor. What no one saw was the emotional hangover she suffered nightly ~ the crying in the car, the inability to sleep, the existential dread of a single typo.

When her therapist asked her to journal not about her achievements, but about her anger, Carla froze. Anger had no place in her polished persona (#PersonaWork). It was impolite. Unsafe. Unwelcome.

But behind the curtain of perfection lived a smouldering grief ~ an inner child who was only praised when she performed, never when she rested. Anger was the shadowed part of her humanity she had disowned. In time, she began naming the small betrayals she tolerated: when she said yes but meant no, when she smiled while shrinking.

Through conscious boundary setting, nervous system support, and emotional honesty (#EmotionalHonesty), Carla realized rest wasn't weakness. It was her act of resistance. And slowly, her identity stopped being built on burnout and started being shaped by truth.

Snapshot 2: The Man Who Always Needed Control

Theme: Relational Triggers + Core Wounds (#Triggers #RelationalHealing)

Darren prided himself on being rational, grounded, and logical. His friends said he had a calming presence, but in relationships, things always unravelled. When his girlfriend made decisions without him or arrived home later than expected, his heart rate would spike. Words he didn't mean would pour out, followed by cold silences. He told himself he just liked structure. But structure was not the problem ~ emotional chaos was. And it terrified him.

During somatic therapy (#SomaticWork), a guided exercise asked him to describe the bodily sensation of being "out of control." His chest ached. His jaw clenched. And then ~ without warning ~ he cried. In those tears was a memory: being eight years old, hiding in the closet as his parents argued violently in the kitchen. Back then, control meant survival. And now, it was sabotaging his intimacy. Through breathwork, shadow integration (#ShadowArmor), and deep accountability, Darren began to recognize that the panic wasn't about the present moment ~ it was the past calling for resolution. And he answered, not with blame, but with compassion.

Snapshot 3: The Woman Who Couldn't Stop Giving

Theme: Co-dependency + Disowned Needs (#Co-dependency #SelfWorth)

Meera was loved by everyone ~ or so it seemed. She organized birthdays, brought meals to sick friends, and always picked up the slack. But at night, she would lie awake wondering why no one ever did the same for her. She'd resent people for not checking in, then feel guilty for being resentful. When she started therapy, she described herself as "selfless." Her therapist gently asked, "What if your giving is how you hide?" That question cracked something open.

88

Meera was the eldest daughter of emotionally immature parents. She learned early that love had to be earned through usefulness. Her own needs were dismissed, so she dismissed them too. She wasn't kind because she was overflowing ~ she was kind because she was starving. Shadow work (#SelfDiscovery) helped her meet the parts of herself that had always longed to be seen without performance. She began experimenting with small no's, with silence, with being unavailable. It felt terrifying ~ and revolutionary. Over time, she realized that being loved for who she was, not what she did, was the medicine she never thought she deserved.

Snapshot 4: The Teen Who Was Always Angry

Theme: Intergenerational Trauma + Firefighter Parts (#AncestralShadow #TraumaAwareness)

Jax was sixteen and already a regular in the principal's office. He'd been suspended twice, skipped classes, and once punched a locker until his knuckles bled. Most adults called him disrespectful, aggressive, even dangerous. But beneath the rage was a silence that refused to speak unless someone actually listened. When he finally saw a trauma-informed youth therapist, the first thing she said was, "I'm not afraid of your anger." And that's when he wept.

For the first time, someone saw beyond the behaviour. Jax wasn't angry for no reason. His father had vanished before he could speak. His mother cycled through abusive partners. Jax's nervous system had been living in fight-or-flight for years. His "anger" was a Firefighter part (#FirefighterParts) ~ an emotional emergency system designed to keep pain out of reach. Through trauma-informed care, journaling, and storytelling, Jax began to name the emotions he didn't yet have language for. He wasn't broken. He was armoured. And underneath all that armor was a boy who wanted to be safe enough to trust love again.

Snapshot 5: The Mother Who Was Never Enough

Theme: Projection + Ancestral Expectations (#Projection #MotherWound)

Elena loved her daughter, truly. But when her child cried over small things or needed constant comfort, something inside her would tighten. "You need to toughen up," she'd say, almost on reflex.

At night, she'd cry in guilt. She wasn't trying to be cruel ~ she just didn't understand why it bothered her so deeply. In a parenting support circle rooted in parts work (#PartsWork), a facilitator asked her to sit with the question, "What does your daughter's pain remind you of?"

It hit her like a wave. Her daughter reminded her of herself ~ her softness, her needs, her desire for connection. As a child, Elena was raised by stoic immigrants who believed emotion was weakness. Crying was punished, and vulnerability was met with silence. She hadn't just buried her feelings ~ she buried the part of her that felt at all. Her daughter wasn't the problem ~ she was the mirror.

Through journaling, ancestral healing (#AncestralShadow), and conscious reparenting, Elena began to say the words to her child that she had never heard: "It's okay to feel. You're safe. You don't have to earn love here."

Cross-Disciplinary

Neuroscience

Why the Shadow Lives in the Body

Modern neuroscience confirms what ancient mystics and depth psychologists have long suspected: the body stores what the mind cannot process. When we suppress emotion ~ whether fear, shame, or grief ~ it doesn't simply vanish. It finds refuge in muscle tension, nervous system patterns, and hormonal feedback loops.

The amygdala, the brain's fear centre, lights up when we encounter emotional memories or threats ~ real or perceived. This helps explain why "triggers" (#Triggers) can feel so overwhelming: the body thinks it's reliving the past. Practices like breathwork, EMDR, vagus nerve stimulation, and somatic experiencing help bring these frozen shadows back into motion ~ where they can be seen, felt, and released. In shadow work, the body becomes both a map and a doorway.

Mythology

Meeting the Minotaur Within

In Greek mythology, the Minotaur ~ half-man, half-beast ~ lives hidden in a labyrinth. It is a creature both feared and misunderstood. Many shadow work practitioners see this tale as symbolic: the labyrinth is the psyche, and the Minotaur is the shadow ~ wild, repressed, and exiled to the unconscious. Only by entering the maze with intention (like Theseus with his thread) can we confront and understand the parts of ourselves we've been taught to fear.

In Jungian terms, this is the process of *individuation* ~ facing the dark to discover your truth. The monsters aren't there to destroy you. They are aspects of your strength, misdirected by pain. Myth allows us to engage the shadow without pathologizing it. The stories remind us: the darkness holds power ~ but only if we dare to face it.

Spirituality

Integration as Sacred Work

In many Eastern traditions, enlightenment isn't about perfection ~ it's about presence. In Buddhism, for example, the idea of "non-attachment" does not mean avoidance ~ it means holding all emotions lightly, without letting them define us. The shadow, then, is not a flaw to be exorcised but a teacher to be honored (#SelfDiscovery).

Practices like meditation, mantra repetition, and mindfulness help us recognize the constant mental stories we believe ~ and offer us enough distance to question them. From a spiritual lens, shadow work is the soul's path to wholeness. It is not about transcendence but embodied truth. You're not here to bypass your pain ~ you're here to walk with it, as both student and guide.

Cultural Analysis

The Collective Shadow in Modern Times

In psychological terms, the shadow is often personal. But on a broader scale, every society has a collective shadow (#CollectiveShadow): the traits, truths, or behaviours it refuses to acknowledge. In some cultures, it may be emotional expression. In others, racial inequality, ecological destruction, or gender nonconformity.

When unacknowledged, the collective shadow festers ~ emerging as social division, moral superiority, or systemic harm. Shadow work is not only self-care ~ it is social awareness. When you do your own work, you become less reactive, more accountable, and more capable of change that extends beyond yourself. Cultural healing begins when enough individuals are brave enough to turn inward.

Psychology + Parts Work

From Fragmentation to Compassion

Traditional psychology once viewed "parts" as pathological (as in dissociative identity disorder). Today, through frameworks like Internal Family Systems (IFS), we recognize that *everyone* has parts ~ inner critics, wounded children, protectors, rebels. These aren't defects ~ they're strategies.

When these parts operate unconsciously, they can sabotage us. When brought into conscious relationship with our Core Self (#CoreSelf), they become powerful allies. Instead of trying to fix yourself, parts work asks: What if every part of you makes sense? What if you're already whole ~ and just waiting to be heard?

93

FAQs
Shadow Work

Demystifying Common Questions
About the Inner Journey

Q1: What exactly is shadow work, and how do you explain it to someone new?

Shadow work is the intentional practice of facing the parts of yourself that you've hidden, denied, or suppressed ~ often unconsciously. These might be traits, feelings, or memories you were taught were "too much," "not enough," or simply unacceptable. Coined by Carl Gustav Jung, the "shadow" is not evil ~ it is unseen. To do shadow work is to make the unconscious conscious and to meet yourself in your full humanity (#ShadowWork #SelfDiscovery).

It's not a ritual, a trend, or a tool for perfection. It's a process of radical self-honesty and compassion. You're not fixing what's broken ~ you're reclaiming what's been buried. The more you bring your shadow into the light, the less control it has over your life.

Q2: Is shadow work good or bad for you?

Shadow work, when approached responsibly and at the right pace, is deeply beneficial. It helps reduce emotional reactivity, improve relationships, and unlock parts of your identity that have been frozen in time (#EmotionalHealing). However, it *can* feel destabilizing if approached too quickly, without support, or during an emotionally vulnerable season.

It's not "bad" ~ it's just deep. Like clearing out an old wound, there may be discomfort before relief. Think of it not as something dangerous, but as something sacred that requires awareness, grounding, and gentleness (#HealingJourney).

Q3: Do therapists recommend shadow work?

Yes ~ many therapists who work in depth psychology, parts work (like IFS), somatic therapy, and trauma-informed models are strong advocates of shadow integration (#ShadowIntegration). While not all therapists will use the term "shadow," many support its core practice: acknowledging unconscious patterns, embracing emotional honesty, and restoring inner balance.

If you're already in therapy, speak to your practitioner about incorporating shadow work themes. Many frameworks already include it under different names: inner child work, reparenting, emotional processing, and parts dialogue (#InnerWork #TherapyTools).

Q4: Why do people avoid shadow work?

Because it's easier to cling to who we think we *should* be than to face who we really are. Shadow work threatens the illusion of control. It invites us to examine uncomfortable truths: jealousy, anger, shame, unmet needs, and unhealed wounds. Most of us have built identities that depend on hiding these parts.

Avoidance often comes from fear ~ of being overwhelmed, judged, or broken beyond repair. But you are not too much. You are not too damaged. You are simply layered. Avoiding the shadow

95

doesn't make it disappear ~ it just lets it steer your life from the dark (#SelfAwareness #EmotionalBravery).

Q5: What is an example of shadow work in practice?

Let's say you're constantly annoyed by a friend's neediness. You judge them. You avoid them. But instead of blaming them, you turn inward and ask: *Why does their vulnerability bother me so much?* Maybe it's because you weren't allowed to express your own needs growing up. Maybe their emotional openness activates your disowned grief.

Shadow work means turning the mirror around. You might journal this, trace it back to a core memory, and begin speaking to that inner part of you ~ the one who still longs to be held. That's not just insight ~ it's integration (#TriggerWork #PartsWork).

Q6: How do I do the shadowing technique or method?

There's no single formula, but here are powerful entry points:

- ➤ Journaling: Ask yourself questions like, What do I criticize in others? What do I fear people seeing in me?
- ➤ Dreamwork: Pay attention to recurring dreams or symbols ~ your unconscious is already speaking.
- ➤ Somatic tracking: Notice where emotion lives in your body and breathe into it.
- ➤ Parts dialogue: Speak to the "part" of you that feels rejected or reactive. Listen without judgment.

You don't need to conquer the shadow ~ you need to *relate* to it. Over time, you'll recognize when you're acting from a triggered part, and when you're responding from your whole self (#SelfDiscovery #EmotionalMaturity).

Q7: How do I use the shadow method in daily life?

Start with curiosity over control. When you're triggered, pause and ask: *What is this really about?* When you find yourself overreacting, ask: *Who inside me is afraid right now?* When you notice envy, ask: *What desire have I silenced in myself?*

Shadow work in daily life looks like slowing down, telling the truth, and sitting with what you usually avoid. It's the art of noticing patterns and bringing warmth, not shame, to the parts of you that still ache (#SelfTransformation #GrowthMindset).

Reflection Questions for Practitioners & Educators

Supporting Conscious Facilitation and Shadow-Informed Practice

"Knowing your own darkness is the best method for dealing with the darknesses of other people." ~ *Carl Gustav Jung*

Group 1: Self-Awareness and Inner Relationship

#SelfAwareness #PersonalIntegrity

1) What is your own relationship to your shadow? Before we guide others into their depths, we must understand our own. Which emotional patterns still feel unacceptable to you? Which traits do you hide behind professionalism, busyness, or confidence? The parts you haven't made peace with will often rise up when working with someone who activates them. If you haven't brought compassion to your inner critic, your guidance might carry judgment instead of presence. This isn't about perfection ~ it's about courageous self-awareness.

2) Where do you notice resistance in your work with others? Resistance isn't always theirs. Sometimes, your fatigue, frustration, or control tendencies are reflections of your own emotional limits. Do certain types of sessions drain you more than others? Are you subtly avoiding particular conversations? Resistance is not the

enemy ~ it's a signpost. What might it be asking you to witness or honor in yourself?

3) How do you respond when someone mirrors a part of you you've rejected? If a client is emotionally needy, do you feel tight or judgmental? If a student is rebellious, do you double down on authority? Often, those we struggle to support are reflecting a younger, exiled version of ourselves. By welcoming their expression, you also open a door to self-repair. What part of you is being called back to the circle?

4) Are there "types" of clients or students you unconsciously favour or avoid? Who gets your most generous attention? Who frustrates you the most? Your preferences and blind spots are maps to your own shadow. Are you only comfortable with "high performers"? Do you struggle with emotional outbursts, silence, or need for clarity? Notice where you lean in ~ and where you subtly pull away.

5) What do you do when you make a mistake in your session or space? Do you name it? Apologize? Over-explain? Withdraw? Your ability to own imperfection without spiralling into shame is a powerful model for those you support. Shadow-integrated practitioners know that repair is more valuable than performance. Mistakes don't diminish your credibility ~ they deepen your humanity.

Group 2: Power, Language, and Ethical Presence

#LanguageMatters #FacilitatorEthics

6) What language do you use to describe emotions, trauma, or "blocks"? Words shape reality. When you say someone is "resistant" or "stuck," do you create a judgment or offer insight? Do you call their patterns "self-sabotage," or do you ask what part of them is still afraid? Shadow-informed work avoids pathologizing language. Choose words that open doors, not reinforce shame.

7) How do you support integration ~ not just revelation? Breakthroughs are powerful, but what happens after the tears, the aha moments, the energetic shifts? Do you check in a week later? Do you offer tools for grounding or rest? Integration is where real transformation happens. Make space for digestion, not just expression.

8) Do you unintentionally reward performative growth? Are you praising the loudest breakthroughs and overlooking the quiet process of showing up? Not all healing looks cinematic. Sometimes the most courageous act is simply sitting in discomfort without retreating. Let your spaces honor slow bloomers and emotional stillness too.

9) How do you frame vulnerability in your space? Do you celebrate tears but subtly withdraw from anger? Do you equate openness with spiritual progress? Be mindful that you're not demanding emotional exposure as proof of growth. True vulnerability isn't performance ~ it's safety, and it must be chosen, not coerced.

10) Do your policies, pricing, or boundaries reflect both sustainability and care? Is your work accessible? Do your boundaries support your longevity and integrity? If you're over-giving or under-charging, resentment can sneak in. If you're rigid or distant, trust may erode. Ethical facilitation lives in the balance between care for self and care for others.

Group 3: Relational Dynamics and Co-Regulation

#CompassionFatigue #CoRegulation #NervousSystemSupport

11) How do you recognize when transference or projection is occurring? Are you being seen clearly ~ or are you becoming a stand-in for a parent, authority figure, or old wound? What parts of you light up when this happens? Can you stay grounded, or do you feel compelled to fix, prove, or withdraw? Naming projection in yourself and others is a vital step in holding ethical space.

12) How do you care for your nervous system before and after deep sessions? Do you prepare yourself with intention? Do you decompress afterward? The body of the facilitator is a tuning fork for the entire room. If you're holding tension, it ripples. If you're regulated, it soothes. Self-regulation is not indulgent ~ it's professional readiness.

13) What happens internally when someone challenges your ideas or approach? Do you feel threatened, dismissed, or defensive? Can you hold space for disagreement without collapse? Shadow work requires that we drop our ego attachment to being the "knower." Being open to challenge is part of being trauma-informed and human.

14) Do you feel responsible for the outcome of someone else's healing? The desire to help can sometimes slide into over-responsibility. If you're exhausted or disappointed when someone doesn't "break through," ask: What part of me needs their progress to validate my worth? Empowerment means trusting their pace ~ not controlling their process.

15) How do you distinguish between holding space and emotional labour? There's a difference between creating safety and absorbing pain. Are you emotionally recovering for days after each session? Are you carrying others' trauma in your body? Burnout is often a sign of poor energetic hygiene. Support others without abandoning yourself.

Group 4: Cultural and Collective Awareness

#CollectiveShadow #CulturalSensitivity #AncestralHealing

16) How do you honor cultural, ancestral, or systemic layers of the shadow? Shadow work isn't just individual. It's ancestral. It's cultural. Do your methods acknowledge generational trauma, colonization, and collective grief? Do your tools leave space for rage, displacement, and inherited wounds that aren't yours alone?

17) Have you explored your own biases and social conditioning through shadow work? Everyone has cultural programming ~ about race, gender, ability, class. What have you internalized? What do you fear saying? What assumptions do you carry into your sessions? Anti-oppression work is shadow work.

18) How do you handle privilege and power in your role? If you're in a position of authority, trust, or influence ~ how do you use it? Do you name your privilege or hide behind spiritual neutrality? Do you share power or centre yourself? Humility is part of integration.

19) Are you creating space for collective grief and cultural repair? Are your circles only centred on individual breakthroughs, or do they allow for community pain, social justice reflection, and systemic healing? Sometimes shadow work means sitting in discomfort that isn't yours ~ but is yours to witness.

20) What assumptions do you bring into the room based on someone's identity? Do you expect certain clients to be "strong," "emotional," "quiet," or "resilient"? How do these assumptions affect your tone, expectations, or silence? What unspoken stereotypes still live in your unconscious?

Appendix

Ethics of Shadow Work: Navigating Responsibility, Power And Psychological Integrity

Shadow Work Is Not a Trend ~ It's a Responsibility

Shadow work has entered mainstream language, spiritual spaces, and online coaching circles with unprecedented speed. While the rising popularity signals a cultural hunger for inner truth and emotional authenticity, it also raises a critical question: *Who is holding this space ~ and how well are they holding it?*

Shadow work is not a casual practice. It is not entertainment. It is not something to prescribe from a script. It is a deep psychological and emotional process that invites individuals to face grief, anger, shame, trauma, projection, fear, and buried identity. When this work is guided without care ~ or marketed without boundaries ~ it can cause harm. That harm might look like emotional flooding, re-traumatization, misdiagnosis, spiritual bypassing, or an increased sense of isolation and fragmentation.

This appendix is not a set of rules. It's an invitation to move with integrity.

1. Trauma Awareness Is Non-Negotiable

#TraumaInformed #NervousSystemHealing

Working with the shadow means working with trauma, even if unspoken. Any facilitator, coach, or educator inviting others to do shadow work must be trauma aware. This means understanding how the nervous system stores survival responses, recognizing signs of dissociation, knowing when to pause, and having a referral network of licensed professionals.

You do not need to be a therapist to hold space. But you *do* need to know when you are out of your depth ~ and when someone else's healing needs to happen in a clinically supported container.

2. The Facilitator Must Know Their Own Shadow

#SelfAwareness #EmbodiedLeadership

It is unethical to guide others into emotional spaces you have not navigated yourself. Without personal shadow integration, projection becomes inevitable. Unmet needs for power, control, admiration, or emotional rescue can leak into sessions and group spaces, often under the guise of "service" or "intuition."

Practitioners who do not consistently engage with their own unconscious patterns risk becoming spiritual narcissists or emotional by-passers. True integrity comes from being a student of your own shadow before becoming a guide for anyone else's.

3. Language Shapes the Healing Space

#LanguageMatters #EmpowermentNotShame

Using shame-laden or binary language ~ such as "low vibration," "not doing the work," or "resistant energy" ~ can reinforce trauma. Ethical shadow work requires language that is inclusive, curious, and non-diagnostic. The goal is not to label the client but to create a container where complexity can safely emerge.

Use metaphors that soften and illuminate, not ones that punish or prescribe. Words should invite people deeper into themselves, not push them further into judgment.

4. Power Must Be Acknowledged, Not Denied

#PowerDynamics #FacilitatorEthics

Whether you are a therapist, coach, spiritual mentor, or educator ~ your role carries power. That power must be held with responsibility. The moment you deny your influence, you become dangerous. In shadow work, people are vulnerable. They are raw. They may unconsciously place you in the role of healer, parent, or authority.

If you are not conscious of your power, you will misuse it. Ethical space-holders are transparent, given boundaries, and self-reflective. They are willing to be challenged and open to feedback. They do not claim superiority or spiritual hierarchy.

5. Integration Is More Important Than Insight

#HealingJourney #IntegrationOverBreakthrough

Emotional breakthroughs are only the beginning. Ethical facilitators understand that true healing happens *after* the session ~ in the quiet hours when a person is trying to make sense of what just opened inside them. Do you offer aftercare practices? Do you create room for follow-up? Do you remind your clients or community that the goal is not to be "done" ~ but to be present?

Without integration, shadow work becomes spiritual tourism. We do not visit our pain just to leave it behind ~ we build a home that can hold it.

6. Collective Context Cannot Be Ignored

#CollectiveHealing #CulturalSensitivity

Much of what we call shadow is not just personal ~ it's cultural, ancestral, systemic. Practitioners must understand that people do not arrive in your space as blank slates. They bring inherited trauma, cultural wounds, religious shame, economic fear, neurodivergence, and gendered expectations.

Your work must be able to hold these complexities. If not, you risk retraumatizing people by telling them their shadow is "resistance" when in fact it may be oppression or erasure. Inclusion is not a trend. It is a fundamental principle of ethical healing.

7. Do Not Over-Promise

#SafeSpace #EmotionalIntegrity

Shadow work is not a fix. It's not a quick transformation. It is not a path to instant abundance, perfect relationships, or spiritual bliss. Be wary of marketing that promises too much. Ethical shadow guides don't guarantee outcomes ~ they create space for emergence.

Never tell someone you can "clear" or "heal" their shadow for them. That promise undermines their agency and creates false dependence. The true work lies within them ~ not in you.

8. You Are Not the Answer ~ You Are a Mirror

#EthicalFacilitation #SacredSpace

As a practitioner, your job is not to solve or save. Your job is to witness. To reflect. To ask brave questions and hold brave silences. To remind the person in front of you that they already carry the wisdom they need ~ they just forgot how to hear it.

Shadow work is sacred not because it fixes people, but because it invites them to love themselves in the places no one else ever could. Be the mirror. Not the map.

Foundational Findings in Shadow Psychology

A Reflection on Jungian Roots and Evolving Psychological Thought

#CarlJung #ShadowWork #DepthPsychology #InnerWork

Carl Gustav Jung: The Origin of the Shadow Archetype

Carl Gustav Jung, Swiss psychiatrist and founder of Analytical Psychology, introduced the concept of the shadow as one of the core archetypes of the human psyche. According to Jung, the shadow consists of the unconscious parts of the personality that the conscious ego does not identify with—often traits we suppress, deny, or disown.

Jung did not see the shadow as merely negative. In fact, he believed that confronting and integrating these hidden parts of ourselves was essential for **individuation**, the process of becoming a whole and authentic self.

Core findings from Jung's work:

➢ "The shadow is a moral problem that challenges the whole ego-personality, for no one can become conscious of the shadow without considerable moral effort."
➢ Unacknowledged shadow aspects often lead to projection, judgment, or internal conflict.

- ➤ Integration requires not eradication but recognition and acceptance.
- ➤ Only by facing our shadow can we move toward authenticity, emotional maturity, and inner peace.

Post-Jungian Thinkers and Expansions

Many psychologists and theorists have expanded upon Jung's concept of the shadow, contextualizing it within modern frameworks of trauma, identity, and relational psychology.

James Hillman
Archetypal Psychology

Hillman reframed Jungian ideas through a mythopoetic lens. He emphasized the soul's need for depth, image, and symbolic expression. He believed the shadow was not to be "cured" but befriended, woven into the aesthetic and narrative of the inner world.

- ➤ Hillman encouraged symbolic imagination and inner dialogue with shadow parts.
- ➤ He saw pathology not as something to fix, but as a potential source of meaning.

Robert A. Johnson
Shadow and Gold

In books like *Owning Your Own Shadow*, Johnson made Jung's complex ideas accessible to the public.

➢ He emphasized the balance of opposites, how the shadow holds both darkness and gold.
➢ He wrote that "wherever one's shadow is, there also is one's power."

Marie-Louise von Franz
Jung's Disciple and Dream Analyst

A close collaborator of Jung, von Franz delved deeply into dreams, fairy tales, and myth. She wrote that shadow material often appears symbolically first, through images, stories, or figures in dreams.

➢ She emphasized the symbolic language of the unconscious.
➢ She maintained that only through close attention to personal and collective myths can we understand the psyche.

John Beebe
Shadow and the Typological Self

Beebe integrated Jungian shadow theory into psychological type theory, emphasizing how each person's shadow is connected to their inferior and unconscious functions.

➢ He saw the shadow not as one single entity, but a system of archetypes that mirror the personality type's blind spots.
➢ His work brought a structural, integrative lens to shadow theory.

Clarissa Pinkola Estés
Women Who Run with the Wolves

Though a Jungian analyst and storyteller, Estés brought deep cultural and feminine insight into the shadow.

- ➤ She emphasized storytelling, ritual, and deep listening as forms of integration.
- ➤ The shadow is portrayed not as pathology, but as a powerful teacher when approached with reverence.

Contemporary Integration:
The Intersection of Jungian Thought
and Trauma Theory

Today, Jung's shadow concept is being re-evaluated in the context of:

- ➤ **Trauma-informed care**: Understanding how parts of the shadow are protective adaptations, not moral failings.
- ➤ **Neuroscience**: Recognizing that shadow material is often stored somatically and can be re-integrated through body-based practices.
- ➤ **Social and cultural psychology**: Expanding shadow work to include inherited trauma, systemic oppression, and identity fragmentation.

Shadow work is not about healing in the traditional sense; it is about wholeness. It is about honoring complexity, integrating contradiction, and making space for what has been silenced.

Jung believed that the path to enlightenment did not require fleeing the dark but embracing it. The evolution of shadow psychology over the past century has only deepened this truth. As we continue into an era of collective awakening and inner accountability, shadow work stands not as a trend, but as a timeless compass for the human soul.

Continue the Journey

You have arrived at the close of this book ~ but not the end of the work.

Shadow work is not a task to complete or a checklist to conquer. It is a lifelong process of remembering, releasing, reclaiming, and integrating. As you continue on your path, know that you are not alone. Millions across the globe are walking beside you ~ some quietly, some bravely, and many in between. What unites them is not perfection, but willingness.

You may revisit this book in different seasons of your life. Each return will reveal something new ~ not because the text has changed, but because *you* have.

The hashtags embedded throughout this book are not mere decoration. They represent some of the most widely used and resonant psychological and spiritual search terms of 2025. If you are drawn to deepen your understanding or explore community reflections, you are invited to use these hashtags on platforms like Instagram, TikTok, Pinterest, YouTube, and online search engines. They offer a gateway to real-time dialogue, practitioner insights, and collective healing narratives.

Let these tags serve as stepping stones into deeper spaces ~ but return often to your inner knowing. No trend, no teacher, no technique is wiser than the truth that already lives inside you.

Shadow Work AI Companion

Your shadow journey doesn't have to end when you put the book down. To support deeper reflection and personal exploration, you now have access to the **Shadow Work AI Companion** – an interactive guide built around the same principles of Jung, Freud, and the evolving practice of shadow integration.

This tool is designed to help you:

- Ask personalised questions about shadow work, inner healing, and self-integration
- Receive thoughtful, reflective guidance in real time
- Explore journaling prompts, emotional triggers, and archetypal patterns in more depth
- Continue your practice privately, at your own pace

Simply scan the QR code below:

Use it as a companion while reading, or return to it whenever you need a mirror for your inner journey. Thousands are already using AI to illuminate their shadow self - this is your chance to join them.

www.ingramcontent.com/pod-product-compliance
Lightning Source LLC
Chambersburg PA
CBHW070334090426
42733CB00012B/2470